Ma Frump's
Cultural Guide to
Instant Intellectualism

Illustrations by Louann Jordan

---

the sunstone press

Santa Fe, New Mexico / 1973

Copyright © 1973 By Marcia Muth Miller

ISBN: 0-913270-17-2

FIRST EDITION

Book Design By Douglas J. Houston

Photograph of Ma Frump taken by Beverly Gile

Printed in the United States of America by Starline, Albuquerque, New Mexico

DEDICATED TO

Jimmy Smith — the most instant
intellectual I ever met.

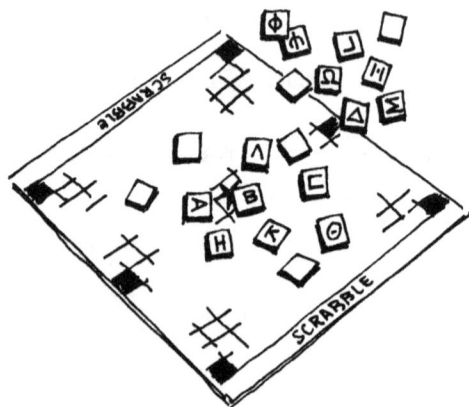

TABLE OF CONTENTS

...in a SHAKESPEARE COLORING BOOK

WHY INTELLECTUALISM?

Why intellectualism, you may well ask. And, my answer would have to be — why not? Isn't it the "in" thing now? This is especially true for us ladies. Intellectualism is certainly a part of the women's liberation movement and you don't want to have an old-fashioned image in a new world. On the other hand, the pressure to be an intellectual is not just on women — no, men are under the same obligation to present a facade of intellectualism to a curious and waiting world.

Unfortunately, there are many interesting things to do today that are vastly more relaxing and entertaining than the serious pursuit of knowledge. However, you can, by following my book, "bake your cake and eat it too." You can become an instant intellectual in a matter of a few hours (two hours?). Your family and your friends will be astonished. You will be pleased and not at all exhausted by tiresome mental effort.

Instant intellectualism is for the modern individual who would rather be happy than to think deep thoughts!

TRAVEL AND INTELLECTUALISM

Travel plays a great part in your intellectual image but does present some problems. The very word "travel" implies being away from home. Now, of course, if you want to leave home that is fine but if, like me, you hate to be away from the comfort of your daily surroundings then you must use travel in a slightly different way. However, if you feel that you must actually travel, go on tours. A good tour will give you the maximum sights with a minimum of effort.

You can explain not traveling by a variety of intellectual excuses such as "The countries aren't what they used to be"; "With my delicate constitution, I rarely visit foreign lands", or "I feel that it is more patriotic to stay home!" Personally, I feel that a trip every five or ten years is enough. By the judicious use of references to your trip, you can get several years of intellectual use out of one three-week jaunt.

It is possible to keep up on foreign places (that is, any place outside your immediate area) by reading the *National Geographic* regularly. Also make the most of the travels that your friends take. Read their travel brochures, look at their pictures and listen to their stories. When four of my friends went to Africa the same year, I found that I soon knew as much about traveling there as they did and without the inconvenience of leaving home!

It is a help to your intellectual image if you acquire and use a few stock travel phrases. Be sure to refer to "my travel agent" and sprinkle your conversation with vague references to foreign places. Remember you do not need to have been there yourself to be able to say such things as "The Masai warriors are still rather aggressive toward strangers, a kind of provincialism that has ceased in this country." If you have traveled you can always start sentences with such phrases as, "When I was in _____", "My guide in _____ said", "There was this charming restaurant in _____", or "The food is very good (very bad) in _____".

When you travel be sure to get souvenirs of your trip. These souvenirs you can use to decorate your home. This is then another credit to your intellectual image. An African sculpture, a German beer stein, some English china, lace from France or an Indian drum from the Far West gives your home that cosmopolitan air that makes you the intellectual you are.

Of course, you can go a step further and wear a foreign costume when you have guests. This is one way to call attention to your travels and even the most blasé of your guests will take notice of you.

Try to select a costume that is becoming to you. You may only look ridiculous in a grass skirt or an Indian blanket.

Another part of your intellectual travel image is in planning your trip. This can go on for a long time. Select an area or country. Get a lot of brochures and maps from your favorite travel agent. Display these items in careless disarray on your coffee table. Invest in one of those small books for travelers that has all the necessary foreign words in it. The more exotic the language (Swahili or Japanese) the more intellectual you will seem. Get books from the library on the country. The total effect will be one of intense intellectual preparation.

If you pick one of the more unstable parts of the globe, you may never have to actually take the trip since you can depend on a political upheaval to occur and end casual traveling in that area.

To travel or not to travel is something that you will have to decide for yourself. My only advice would be for you to add up the comforts of home plus the discomforts of being away. Remember the natives rarely speak your language and such staple items as hot fudge sundaes are almost unknown once you leave the continental United States.

It takes only a little effort to become a seasoned "armchair" traveler. I can also predict that your friends are often so busy with their own travels that they will not realize that you have not actually left home if you learn to talk a good travel lingo!

FOREIGN WORDS AND PHRASES

Foreign words and phrases add to your intellectual image. You only need to know a few words. There's no problem about when to use them — just sprinkle them into your conversation in the same way you add seasoning to your food!

For your convenience, I have listed a few handy words and phrases and their meanings. Be sure to learn the meanings as you don't want to use the wrong word at the right time.

FRENCH

au courant (**not** au current) — Up-to-date.
casserole — A good way to use leftovers.
c'est la vie — That's life!
cul-de-sac — Dead end.
déjà vu — When you think you've already been through it all before.
de luxe — First rate.
de trop — Too much of a good thing.
en masse — A lot of people.
en route — On the road.
entre nous — Just between us two.
entre trois — Just between us three.
esprit de corps — Everybody's feeling happy.
fait accompli — It's all over.
faux pas — A stupid mistake.
haute couture — High style.
joyeux Noël — Merry Christmas.
ménage à trois — The basic plot of "R" rated movies.
objet d'art — Any little thing that looks nice, but isn't very useful.
passé — Out-of-date.

LATIN

habeas corpus — Here is the body. (This is useful when discussing mystery stories).
ipso facto — That's the way it is!
magnum opus — The greatest.
mea culpa — It's all my fault.
modus operandi — The way it's done.
persona grata — Someone you like.
persona non grata — Someone you don't like.

ITALIAN

che sarà sarà — That's fate!
la dolce vita — Lot's of fun doing nothing, eating a lot and sleeping late.
prima donna — Someone who acts up and is generally a nuisance.

SPANISH

hasta la vista — Come again.
mi casa es su casa — Make yourself at home.
oro y plata — Lots of money.

GERMAN

auf Wiedersehen — Good-bye.
Donner und Blitz — My goodness!
Gott mit uns — God smiles on us.

I have purposely listed phrases from many languages for they are suitable for various occasions. French is best for garden parties and social evenings. Italian and Spanish phrases can also be used in the evenings. They are also very good when attending sports events. German is a harsher language in tone than the others and should be used sparingly. It is very suitable for the winter months. Latin is impressive. Use it on more formal occasions and during intellectual discussions.

Don't worry about pronounciation. Foreign words always sound funny anyway!

Incidentally, I have given more space to French words and phrases because French was the language of diplomacy in the eighteenth and nineteenth centuries.

APPEARANCE IS FIFTY PERCENT!

Appearance is one-half of the battle in building and maintaining your intellectual image. There are a few simple things that you can do which will automatically make people exclaim when they see you, "That's an intellectual?"

Glasses, of course, are a must. After all, a pair of glasses not only implies literacy but a rather scholarly attitude. You can increase the effect by having more than one pair of glasses. Have one for close work, one for distance, etc. Don't worry if you don't actually need glasses, just buy some with clear glass in them. Remember that what you are interested in is your intellectual appearance.

There are other uses for your glasses. If you are asked a question and aren't sure of the answer, taking off your glasses and cleaning them gives you the needed pause to collect your thoughts. Glasses are also very useful as a part of your intellectual gesturing. Fiddling with your frames can be distracting to those who are rude enough to attempt to pin you down on some intellectual point.

For men, I recommend that they achieve the desired intellectual appearance by not only wearing glasses, but by growing a beard, neatly trimmed, of course.

Clothes can also be used to enhance your intellectual appearance. Men should wear a tweed jacket with leather elbow patches; women a tweed skirt, cardigan sweater and sensible walking shoes. Fortunately, we do not have to be intellectual all the time so we can wear clothes more suitable for our personalities at least ninety percent of the time!

Keep in mind that your intellectual image is not confined to clothes but also to various accessories. In addition to the glasses already mentioned, you can carry around a book, a literary magazine, or notebook. You may want to occasionally take out a pen and make notes. While you may only be writing a grocery list, a note to the milkman, or a memo to yourself, if you have a slight frown, other people will think that you are writing notes for an important treatise.

I know one lady who wears a green celluloid eyeshade. Her neighbors are convinced that she is an important writer in disguise. This mistaken identity, which she has tried unsuccessfully to deny, has resulted in many invitations to teas and dinner parties. (This shows some of the advantages of an intellectual reputation!)

One further word — if you smoke, try using a long cigarette holder. It's more intellectual than smoking plain cigarettes. A pipe always suggests a scholar but this is for men only; a woman smoking a pipe is apt to be regarded as rather eccentric in her behavior!

LEARNING THE INTELLECTUAL GESTURE

It is not enough, dear readers, to look like an intellectual, you must also act like one. For that purpose, I suggest that you learn a variety of intellectual gestures.

Your glasses should become part of your gesturing equipment. When making a point, take them off and tap them (gently, of course) against the open palm of one hand. When you wish to appear deep in thought, remove your glasses and put the end of one of the bows up to your lips. This is even more effective when accompanied by a faraway look.

You can indicate intellectual distraction by placing your glasses up on your head.

There are other well-known gestures and habits for you to acquire such as the careful cough, the intellectual frown, the enigmatic smile and the lifted eyebrows.

Coughing no longer needs to be confined to days of illness. No, you can use a cough to indicate disagreement with, or suspicion in the validity of another's argument. You do not need to say a word to express your opinion, just cough. In this way you do not really need to have a well-thought out opinion at all. I call this the careful cough because it should be used properly and not at the wrong times or people will merely think you have some kind of an allergy. This discreet little cough is all you ever need to express intellectual disapproval or disbelief in what is being said.

The intellectual frown is a way of visibly indicating the thought process. Frankly, I think it is more becoming to men than women, but it can be used by both sexes.

The enigmatic smile is very useful when you are in a discussion about a subject with which you are unfamiliar. Remember you don't have to stumble around in the conversation, just smile. Let other people wonder just what you mean by that smile!

Lifted eyebrows are a well-known device to indicate surprise, shock and a lot of other responses. Again, you are never at a loss for words because you don't have to speak, you just use appropriate gestures.

And, don't forget your hands. You can convey the idea of deep thought by merely placing a hand on your chin or on your forehead. I suggest that you pick the position that is most becoming to you.

The intellectual gesture when properly used can be your passport into sparkling company!

The Careful Cough

The Intellectual Frown

The Enigmatic Smile

The Lifted Eyebrows

The Hand on Forehead

Glasses with Far Away Look

HOW TO GIVE YOUR HOME
THAT INTELLECTUAL LOOK

There is, you know, such a thing as intellectual decorating and you can do it yourself. By following my few simple suggestions, you can have the experience of having callers say to you (as they say to me) "Well, looking around here I can see just how intellectual you are!"

Buy a world globe. A globe is such an attractive "objet d'art"! Keep it in a prominent place. If helps if you are observed studying it occasionally. Spin it slowly with one finger while you murmer "Hmm" or shake your head solemnly. Incidentally a globe with a light in it makes a nice little night light.

If you don't have room for a globe or don't want to buy one, get a map. Put it up on a wall where it can be seen. If you want to go one step further, put map pins in it. A friend of mine has a reproduction of an old map on his wall. When asked what the pins are, he simply says, "Trade Routes." I myself have a large map of the United States with various colored pins stuck in it. This, I explain, represents "Travels." Does this give you ideas?

You can also decorate with maps of a special nature — maps showing the locale of Shakespeare's plays, Federal Bank depositories, archeological finds or the location of McDonald's hamburger stands. Along with maps, use posters as an intellectual decorative aid. Posters of well-known people or of special events are preferable to posters advertising cigars or dog food. Travel posters are very good. They give an aura of internationalism to your home!

Framed certificates of any kind are valuable. One acquaintance of mine has made it a hobby of hers to snoop around secondhand shops and buy old certificates which she then has tastefully framed.

Signed portraits, especially when your name is mentioned on the picture, are very effective. A friend of mine has decorated an entire wall in her home with pictures of famous writers which she has clipped from book jackets. Her friends are always expressing their amazement at her "portrait gallery."

It is important to have the **right** magazines, books and newspapers in plain view, for you never know when someone might drop in. But, in the privacy of your bedroom you can keep the magazines, books and newspapers that you really enjoy reading — the ones that make you relax instead of think!

On your coffee table you should have *Opera News, The New York Times, The National Observer, The Atlantic, Poetry* and an art magazine. If you wish to further enhance your intellectual image, subscribe to such periodicals as *Journal of Higher Education, Slavic Review, Ecology* and *Classical World. Yachting* is one magazine that looks very nice on display but is questionable if you do not live near water.

Art adds much to your home environment. Have at least one original painting hanging in your house even if it is by your cousin or brother-in-law. It doesn't matter who did the painting, what is important is that it is an "original." And, when questioned about its value, you can truthfully say that it is "priceless."

A small piece of sculpture in a prominent place immediately labels you as a person of artistic stature. Again, if you have a relative or friend who does sculpture, you can easily have an original, otherwise you may have to settle for a reproduction.

Don't worry if your original piece of art looks funny to you or seems a little out of proportion. Most people will accept it if you remember to tell them that it is a unique, one-of-its-kind art object. After all, they will be the ones who notice and look at it. You, who live with it, will quickly get used to it and hardly notice it after the first twenty-four hours.

A suggestion — if visitors seem at a loss for words when viewing your pictures or sculpture, it is only kind and thoughtful to help them along by such phrases as, "Isn't it unique?", "A bit modern but I like it" or "A Renaissance flavor, don't you think?".

Don't forget to use record albums in your intellectual decorating scheme. I recommend only classical music albums. Symphonies, operas and chamber music are the albums to have casually strewn around your living room.

When you have finished reading this section, stop and take a look at your home. Just what impression are you giving? Are you doing all that you can to seem as intellectual as you could be? It's never too late to add those little intellectual decorating touches to your home. The response from your family and friends will amaze you.

Remember you can perform the same kind of intellectual decorating miracles in your home as you were able to do in your garden with the help of my book *MA FRUMP'S CULTURAL GUIDE TO PLASTIC GARDEN-ING.*

You too can have a Ph. D house — one that is a "Perfectly Heavenly Display!"

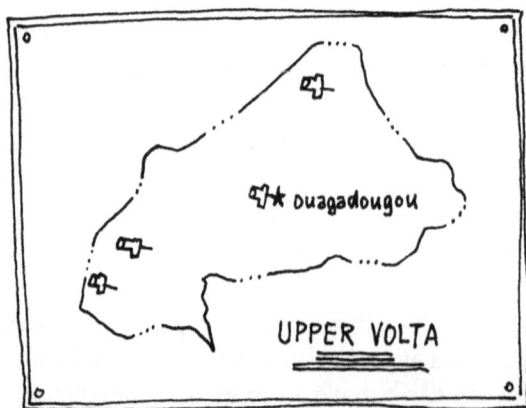

MAKING INTELLECTUAL USE OF YOUR TELEVISION SET AND RADIO

I am always ready to agree that television has great potential as an educating force and cultural center. The documentaries and especially the fine programs on educational television stations are certainly equivalent to attending classes. But, frankly, some of these programs aren't much fun, are they?

Do you feel guilty because you would rather be entertained than educated? Stop, you don't need to! There is an easy way to watch **your** programs and still keep up with **their** programs. Each week buy a TV guide, mark the programs you think you should watch and, incidentally, don't forget to keep track of the programs you will watch. Read the synopsis of the programs in advance, so you will know what you are not watching. Remember that very important programs will be reviewed in the papers so be sure to read those reviews so you can offer intelligent comments on the programs.

Be familiar with the number of the educational channel on your set. You may want to switch channels in a hurry if someone drops in unexpectedly!

Your radio can also help your intellectual image if you have a classical music station in your area. Naturally, I wouldn't expect you to have to listen to that station but you should be able to find it quickly on the dial when an intellectual atmosphere is called for.

A neighbor of mine has an extra radio which she keeps permanently tuned to our FM classical and cultural program station. She simply snaps it on when callers come.

Would you like a few hours of uninterrupted relaxation? Just tell your friends and family that you don't want to be disturbed while you listen to the Metropolitan Opera broadcast on Saturday afternoon. Turn on your radio, put plugs in your ears and settle down with a good mystery book or your favorite magazine.

INTELLECTUAL GAMES

Don't make the mistake of thinking that games have no place in the life of the adult intellectual. In fact, games can become a very important factor in instant intellectualism.

The game that comes most quickly to mind is, of course, chess. Just think a minute – how many homes have you gone into where there is a chess set sitting out in the living room, family room or study? Quite a few, weren't there? Do you think all these people really *play* chess? No, and you can also have the reputation for being a chess player by putting up a chessboard and chess pieces in *your* house.

A word of caution though – do move your chessmen around the board. Leaving them always in the same place is a dead giveaway that you are not really playing. Frankly, I was in one house where the dust was noticeably thick on the chess set!

There is an easy way to "play" chess without the trouble of actually learning. Buy an easy-to-understand book on chess (a book for children is best) and simply place your chessmen according to the diagrams in the book. Be sure to learn the names of all the pieces and some of the common terms like "checkmate."

For your more curious callers, you can either say that you are working out various chess problems yourself or you can imply that you are playing chess via correspondence. If you don't want to be bothered with moving the chess pieces too often, pick an imaginary opponent who lives in a remote area so that there is a long interval between letters and thus the necessity for making moves on the board.

Incidentally, when discussing chess try to avoid talking about it in too specific terms. To add to your chess stature vaguely sprinkle the names "Bobby" and "Boris" in your conversation. Be charmingly mysterious about your chess opponent.

There are other intellectual games. Scrabble can become a real asset to your intellectual image if you buy one of the foreign language Scrabble sets.

Occasionally (when you expect company) put the box out where it can be seen. Or, have it scattered on the table as though you have just finished a game and are putting it away.

When asked about foreign Scrabble, it is safe to say, "It is just a fun way of keeping up on foreign languages."

If you know someone who is well-versed in the particular foreign language of your set, be sure and have your game put away. You wouldn't want to be put in the embarrassing position of playing a game in a language you scarcely know!

There are a number of new games on the market which are social conscience or personality games. They really aren't that much fun and can lead to broken friendships and hurt feelings. However, if you want to be "in", buy one of these games and have it on the shelf. If guests want to play, you can object, saying, "Oh, not that one, it's so passé now!"

Jigsaw puzzles can be used but only if they are of the very complicated variety. Again, you can get by with having one in its unopened box on your bookshelf or table. If asked about the puzzle, you can always imply that you have already worked it, by murmuring, "very difficult". Be sure to remove the cellophane from the box before you talk about having done the puzzle!

If games do not really interest you but you feel that a game should be part of your intellectual equipment, why not pick a game that is no longer popular, or is relatively obscure in your area. You can easily explain your lack of participation in the local bridge club by saying that you only play whist, mahjong or fan-tan.

KEEPING UP WITH LITERATURE

Since literature and intellectualism are somewhat synonymous, you will want to keep up with literature or, in other words, to be *au courant* (see section on Foreign Words and Phrases) with the literary scene.

Because there are thousands of books published each year and you certainly don't want to spend all of your time reading, you will have to look for a better way than "reading" to handle literature. Knowing how to read is one thing, reading is another matter.

You must be selective in your reading choices. The quickest way to instant intellectualism in reading is to confine your reading to book jacket blurbs.

A good book jacket will give you a capsule commentary on the book and some information about the author. You will soon learn how to select the best in book jackets. A really good book jacket is one which also gives you a few remarks from critics as well as a picture of the author.

Browse in your bookstore with notebook and pencil and note down the important information from book jackets. For example, pick out certain key phrases such as "Beautifully written", "Poignant and sensitive" and "Ahead of its time."

There are also certain words and phrases which can be applied to any book. For non-fiction books, I recommend "Scholarly", "he (or she) is certainly to be commended for his (her) research" and "a worthy chronicle". This last is most suitable for a history book. For fiction, "A good characterization", "A splendid setting" and "So timely" are always good.

If you wish to be truly intellectual, you won't want to praise every book jacket you read. No, there are times when it is more proper to take a slightly negative approach. Again there are some words and phrases which are universally suited for all books. In non-fiction try "Poorly re-

searched" or "No bibliography"; in fiction, "No plot" or "It's been done before!" A word of caution, be sure you understand the nature of the book to which you are referring. I once saw a friend reduced to humiliated silence when she mistakenly said "No plot" when questioned about a new cookbook which had a misleading title!

There are two handy words you can use if questioned about a book which you have not yet had a chance to see, "Shocking!" and "Superb." You can choose whether or not you wish to praise or damn a book. If you are alert, you will be able to tell from the tone of your questioner what the popular sentiment is about the book and act accordingly.

A picture of the author on the jacket will help you to develop other comments such as, "He writes well but should really go on a diet", "He certainly looks like a mystery writer" and "She does tell a good story but have you noticed how she dresses?"

In book jacket reading you can choose a particular subject field in which to become an authority or you can develop a wide range of interests.

I personally prefer fiction, but I have a neighbor who is an expert on Chinese history. I must admit that she has an advantage over me for there are fewer books published on Chinese history. I often envy her as I start off to the bookstore to catch up on my reading and she is lounging in her garden.

There are other ways of achieving instant intellectualism in literature. One way is to listen to what other people have to say about books. I call this "the overheard book". Train yourself to pick out key phrases and the gist of plots. However, you can only use this method if you are around people who are in the habit of discussing books.

If you are determined to become **very** intellectual about books you can go a step further and read book reviews that appear in newspapers and magazines. You may even find a favorite reviewer whose opinions you can adopt as your own!

With plenty of time on your hands, you can, of course, go the limit and actually read some books. I recommend condensed books because I am sure you will agree with me that authors use far too many words to express themselves. If you must read books then read only the essence of them. Besides, you can read six condensed books while others are plodding through one whole book.

A word about the classic — classics are books which are here to stay. You should be familiar with at least the best-known classics. You can easily get a list from your local library or better yet, get a reference book which will give you the plots of best-known books. If you are willing to devote an afternoon, you can easily become familiar with the best in the literature of the past.

Advanced "research" in the classics can be done by reading a few encyclopedia articles when you have an hour to spend at the local library. Since your time will be limited, confine yourself to a few authors such as William Shakespeare, Charles Dickens, George Eliot (she was really a woman, you know, so don't make a mistake and talk about "him") and Ralph Waldo Emerson.

But what if you have no time to prepare yourself in literature? Well, there is a way for you too. All you have to do is to shake your head and say "For me there has been no real literature written since the sixteenth century!" This will usually cause a silence to fall while others ponder your statement.

INTELLECTUAL USES OF ASTROLOGY AND ZEN

In recent years, astrology, Zen and certain occult ideas have been the darlings of the intellectual world. Naturally, you don't want to be left out of this "new wave" of thinking and doing. On the other hand, I know that you don't want to spend several hours studying these exotic subjects when you could be watching television or going to a good movie.

All you need to know about astrology, you can learn in an hour. Start by memorizing the signs of the zodiac and their symbols. Next learn the time period for which each sign stands. And, although it takes a little more effort, learn some of the personality characteristics associated with each sign.

Using your astrological knowledge can be fun. When meeting people, ask them their birthday and then you can exclaim, "Ah, so you are a Libra!" (or Gemini, Capricorn, etc.) Then add a sentence or two about some special personality trait. Not the critical or uncomplimentary traits, of course, since you want to make friends, not lose them!

Be sure that you are well-versed in information about your own astrological sign. This can be very useful on certain occasions. For instance, if you are late in arriving for an appointment (or too early), just explain it by saying, "Oh, well, you know I'm a Libra (or other suitable sign) and you know what that means!" And, since a lot of people won't really know what that means but will hesitate to ask, you will be spared any further explanations.

You can also use your astrological sign to excuse your extravagance in buying a new hat, your aversion to exercise, your fondness for ice cream and a thousand other things that might cause occasional comment from your family or friends. After all, who can argue with the stars?

One of the more practical uses of astrology is to predict the day's happenings. Usually, the astrology column in your local newspaper will be satisfactory as an astrological guide. You can use it as a basis for conversation during the day by telling your friends such things as, "Today is a busy day for me as I am expecting an important caller" or "I have to be particularly careful this afternoon so as to not suffer a monetary loss." If you know their zodiac signs, you can also tell your friends what to expect in their day.

If you really want to gain a reputation as a seer, subscribe to an out-of-town paper and use the astrology column in that paper as the basis of your remarks and predictions. Your friends will truly be astonished at what you say!

Tarot cards are very popular but unfortunately difficult to understand and use. However, I would recommend buying a pack anyway. They look

impressive and you can always smile mysteriously and shake your head when someone asks you about them. The impression you want to give is that you understand and respect the Tarot cards but feel too moved to discuss them. The nice thing about Tarot cards is that they are decorative and when you tire of them, you can use them in some artistic way. One of my friends covered a wastebasket with her old Tarot cards and another used them to frame a mirror.

Finally, you can put zip in your life with Zen. Zen has many advantages. To begin with, it is a short word, easy to remember and pronounce. Also, it is very inoffensive and doesn't require any complicated equipment or elaborate rituals.

Since meditation is a part of Zen practice, you will find it an indispensable part of your daily life. Instead of telling your friends that you nap every day after lunch, just say that you set aside an hour a day for your Zen meditation. Your friends will respect you for this attention to metaphysical exercise.

You can also use Zen to explain some of your decisions and attitudes. Just say, "Since Zen, I have felt that _____.", or "I always stop and ask myself, is this compatible with Zen?"

Zen will make you seem to be a more interesting as well as a more intellectual person. Be sure and have one or two books on Zen on your coffee table. I suggest that you get a colored pencil and go through the book underlining certain words or sentences. Also you might write occasional comments in the margin such as, "How true!", "I agree", or "My experience exactly!" You don't need to read the book to do this. Just remember that most authors put the important thing in the first and last paragraphs of each chapter.

Finally, one word that is most frequently used in connection with Zen is the word *koan*. *Koan* means a kind of riddle that has no logical answer. You are supposed to think over these riddles that don't make sense! That gives you an idea of what Zen is all about.

MY INTELLECTUAL DIARY

MY INTELLECTUAL DIARY